W9-AWD-259

A Rabbi Confesses

by
Rabbi Bob Alper
pictures by
Finkstrom

Other Books By Finkstrom Productions:

FREQUENT FLYER FOIBLES

... What's so funny about flying on commercial airlines... LOTS! Especially when you fly the comical skies aboard Knockwurst Airlines. This full-color collection of hilarious cartoons is a *must* for all frequent flyers!

"One thing I know *is* funny is *Frequent Flyer Foibles*...offering us all a wry look at business travel."

Jon Meigs, Publisher
Frequent Flyer Magazine

SOME OF MY BEST FRIENDS ARE JEWISH

...If you're Jewish, are thinking about becoming Jewish or were Jewish in a previous life... this full-color cartoon book is lox of laughs!

A RABBI CONFESSES copyright © 1995 by Finkstrom Publications, LLC.
All rights reserved. No part of this book may be used or reproduced in any manner without written consent except in the case of reprints in the context of reviews.
For information, write: **Finkstrom Productions**
16526 West 78th Street
Suite 340
Eden Prairie, MN 55346
1-800-86-COMIC
(26642)

ATTENTION SCHOOLS AND BUSINESSES:
Finkstrom Productions offers quantity discounts with bulk purchases for educational, business or sales promotional use.

Library of Congress Catalog Card Number: 95-61725

ISBN: 1-888016-18-3

Printed in the U.S.A.

I call this book *A Rabbi Confesses* because, frankly, it's a lot catchier than, say, *Reminiscences from My Years in the Rabbinate* or *Funny Things I Have Noticed About Jews.*

The "confessions" reflect true experiences of a congregational rabbi ---guffaws I could share only with my colleagues and trusted friends until I left full-time synagogue life. Now I can tell everyone!

Much of the book's material is taken directly from my stand-up comedy routine (bookings: call 516-265-2961) and the rest popped up along the way. Every cartoon is absolutely true. Or could be.

I dedicate this book to Sherri and Sherry: Sherri Alper, who encouraged the rabbi she married to follow his dream of becoming a comedian; and Sherry Goodman, my comedy manager, who believed that the idea of a rabbi/stand-up comic had potential when everyone else in the industry told her she was an idiot.

Here it is... PAGE FOUR!

The First Congregational Church

BOX 588, MANCHESTER, VERMONT 05254

Established 1784

To whom it may concern:

I hereby certify that Gentiles will understand at least 97%

of the cartoons in this book.

Very truly,

Richard D. Ringenwald, Sr.

The Rev. Richard D. Ringenwald, Sr.

WHAT THE RABBI SAID...
"YOU'RE RIGHT... I'LL TRY TO SPEND MORE TIME WITH OUR TEENAGERS."
WHAT THE RABBI THOUGHT...
GREAT. FOUR YEARS OF COLLEGE, FIVE IN THE SEMINARY AND A DOCTORAL DEGREE SO I CAN GO BOWLING WITH 14 YEAR-OLDS.
FINKSTROM

"WE NAMED HIM AFTER MY GRANDFATHER. WE CALL HIM... 'GRANDPA'."
FINKSTROM

"... AND NOW, MOVING ALONG TO AGENDA ITEM 57..."
TRUSTEES MEETING
FINKSTROM
"AND I SHALL DWELL IN THE HOUSE OF THE LORD FOREVER."

DO YOU PREFER THE KIBBITZING OR THE NON-KIBBITZING SECTION?
BETH OR SANCTUARY
USHER
FINKSTROM

"WHAT'S CASUAL SEX...
WITHOUT A TIE?"

"I DON'T UNDERSTAND MUCH YIDDISH, BUT I THINK HE LIKED MY SERMON... HE HAD A BROAD SMILE AND USED LOTS OF PHLEGM."
FINKSTROM

...LATE BREAKING BULLETIN
YOU ARE WATCHING THE JEWISH CABLE NEWS NETWORK
"WELCOME.....
.....BELIEVE ME,
YOU DON'T WANT TO KNOW....."

"ACCORDING TO YOUR BLUEPRINTS, WE'LL PRAY FACING SOUTH INSTEAD OF EAST TOWARD JERUSALEM? WELL... AT LEAST WE'LL BE FACING THE LAND OF OUR ANCESTORS... MIAMI!"

"DON'T WORRY, RABBI, YOU'LL BE GREAT... AFTER ALL, YOU'VE HAD TWENTY YEARS EXPERIENCE IN FRONT OF A HOSTILE AUDIENCE."

"THANK YOU FOR CALLING BETH OR... FOR MEMBERSHIP INFORMATION, PRESS ONE... FOR OUR SERVICE SCHEDULE, PRESS TWO... TO COMPLAIN TO THE RABBI, PRESS THREE... TO COMPLAIN **ABOUT** THE RABBI, PRESS FOUR... FIVE... OR SIX."
FINKSTROM

"ONE OF THE JOYS OF THE WINTER HOLIDAY IS LISTENING TO THE T.V. ANCHORS TRYING TO PRONOUNCE CHA-NU-KAH."

"YOU KNOW, RABBI... EACH ONE OF YOUR SERMONS IS BETTER THAN THE NEXT."

"I THINK HE'S THE PATRON SAINT OF FACTORY OUTLET STORES."

I ♥ MY DADDY
"CARL...ENJOY HER WHILE SHE'S STUPID."
FINKSTROM

"TONIGHT'S SPECIAL IS JEWISH CHOW MEIN... THE PORK AND SHELLFISH ARE DICED-UP BEYOND RECOGNITION."
MENU

"HI, THIS IS THE ALPER FAMILY... PLEASE LEAVE YOUR MESSAGE IN A CLEAR, DISTINCT VOICE... BUT NOT SO LOUD THAT YOU WAKE THE DOG."
FINKSTROM

SINGLE JEWISH WOMAN SEEKS SINGLE JEWISH MAN WITH DEAD MOTHER
PERSONAL ADS
FINKSTROM

"AT OUR COLLEGE THEY'VE LUMPED HEBREW, RUSSIAN AND GERMAN TOGETHER...IT'S CALLED THE DEPARTMENT OF SEMITIC AND ANTI-SEMITIC LANGUAGES."
FINKSTROM

"AND THESE ARE OUR CHILDREN...
TAD, DEREK AND CHRISTIE,
AND OUR DOG, YITZCHAK."
FINKSTROM

WELCOME TO
VERMONT
YEAR 'ROUND
JEWISH POPULATION
6000...
SKI SEASON
1.7 MILLION
FINKSTROM

JOYS OF PARENTING
WORKSHOP
"...AND WE DEFINE AGE 16 AS THE 'TERRIBLE TWOS' TIMES EIGHT PLUS A DRIVERS LICENSE."
FINKSTROM

"HE'S VERY HAPPY...ALWAYS WAGGING HIS TAIL. REAL PEPPY GUY... WE NAMED HIM 'PROZAC'."

HANDICAPPED
ENTITLED
$
FINKSTROM

"YOUR EULOGY FOR MY AUNT WAS WONDERFUL. SHE WOULD HAVE LOVED IT... WHAT A SHAME... SHE MISSED IT BY JUST TWO DAYS."

TEL AVIV 24 KM.
CHANGE
EXACT CHANGE
PLEDGES
FINKSTROM

THE RABBI'S REVENGE
"WE NOW INVITE OUR CONGREGATION'S PRESIDENT TO LEAD US IN THE SILENT PRAYER."
FINGERBOW

" NICE TRY, JOEL ... BUT NO, MOSES DID NOT STAY ON THE MOUNTAIN FOR 40 DAYS BECAUSE HE HAD EXTRA LIFT TICKETS."
FINKELBOUL

"THE BIGGEST FIGHT IN OUR DIVORCE WAS OVER WHO GOT TO KEEP OUR THERAPIST."

"IN MY DAY IT WAS DIFFERENT. WE BORROWED TIES FROM OUR FATHERS.. NOT EARRINGS FROM OUR MOTHERS."
FINKSTROM

"OH, YOU'RE JEWISH TOO? AND TO THINK THAT ALL THESE YEARS I'VE BEEN TREATING YOU SO POLITELY!"
FINKSTROM

"NO WATER... NO ELECTRICITY... DOWNWIND FROM THE LATRINE. SHE COULD HAVE THE SAME THRILL JUST BY GOING INTO HER BROTHER'S BEDROOM."

HOW TO TORTURE A RABBI
RABBI...DO YOU REMEMBER MY NAME?
FINKSTROM

"THE SILVERBERGS ARE ORTHODOX... SO THEY HAVE TWO DISHES."
FINKSTROM

"MY WIFE IS LEARNING HYPNOSIS ... NOW I GET NERVOUS WHEN SHE SAYS ANYTHING TWICE."

" I'M NOT SURE WHICH WAY I'M GOING TO VOTE ON THIS ISSUE... BUT I'M PREPARED TO BE BITTER."
BETH OR
TRUSTEES MEETING
ROOM 7
FINKSTROM

THE RABBI & HIS DOG.
"TREIF"
GRRRR!
FINKSTROM
"KOSHER"

CAMP GITCHI-GELT
FOR THE SEVERELY OVERPRIVILEGED
FINKSTROM

"GREAT NEWS, BOB...WE'RE TRADING YOU TO TEMPLE MICAH FOR TWO CANTORS, A MOHEL AND A RABBI TO BE NAMED LATER."
FINKSTROM

"IT'S JUST MOSTLY STUFF PEOPLE DIDN'T WANT HANGING AROUND THE HOUSE... FURNITURE, CLOTHES, APPLIANCES AND THREE RETIRED HUSBANDS."

"NOW THEN... WITH ALL DUE RESPECT TO THE RABBI..."
BOARD MEETING
FINKSTROM
"UH, OH... HERE IT COMES!"

"THIS, THEN, IS THE NUMBER OF YEARS THE JEWISH PEOPLE HAD TO WAIT... BEFORE WE COULD START EATING CHINESE FOOD."

PRESS HERE FOR A MESSAGE FROM THE RABBI
FINKSTROM

"WE WERE ABLE TO ARRANGE A STUDENT LOAN FOR OUR SON... WE'RE LOANING HIM TO A FAMILY IN IOWA."

"HEY BUD... YA' KNOW WHERE I CAN FIND A GOOD KOSHER DELI AROUND HERE?"
FINKSTROM

BETH OR
AMNESTY
PROGRAM
ANYONE RETURNING
MISSING PRAYER BOOKS,
YARMULKAHS
OR LIBRARY BOOKS
CAN EXCHANGE THEM
FOR A
HANDGUN...
NO
QUESTIONS
ASKED.
FINKSTROM

"OH, HELLO, SISTER... I'D LIKE YOU TO MEET MY DAUGHTER... AND, AH, HER LAWYER AND HER ACCOUNTANT."
FINKSTROM

THE RABBI... LONG VIEW
"THE RABBI LOOKS SO SERIOUS... HE MUST BE DEEP IN THOUGHT."
...WITH THE ZOOM LENS
IS THE WAGON DUE FOR LUBE AND OIL?
FINKSTROM

"AND AS YOU CAN SEE, OUR NEW SANCTUARY WILL SLEEP 250 COMFORTABLY."
TEMPLE RENOVATION PROJECT
FINKSTROM

"WHAT ARE YOU... A COMEDIAN?"
CLERGY

"RABBI, YOUR SERMON WAS ABSOLUTELY SUPERFLUOUS."
FINKSTROM

"AND WHEN ONE OF US DIES, I THINK I'LL MOVE TO BOCA."

"I WAITED TEN YEARS FOR A KIDNEY TRANSPLANT... JUST MY LUCK: THE DONOR WAS A BED-WETTER."

"AND SO WE BESTOW UPON THIS CHILD THE HEBREW NAME...SHOSHANAH MALKAH bat LEAH v'SHIMON, AND THE ENGLISH NAME... TIFFANY BRIANNA SPIEGELBERGER."

THE RABBI'S FANTASY
"...AND IN THE SPIRIT OF YOM KIPPUR, IF THERE IS ANYTHING I HAVE SAID OR DONE DURING THE PAST YEAR THAT HAS HURT OR OFFENDED YOU... YOU'RE TOO SENSITIVE."
FINKSTROM